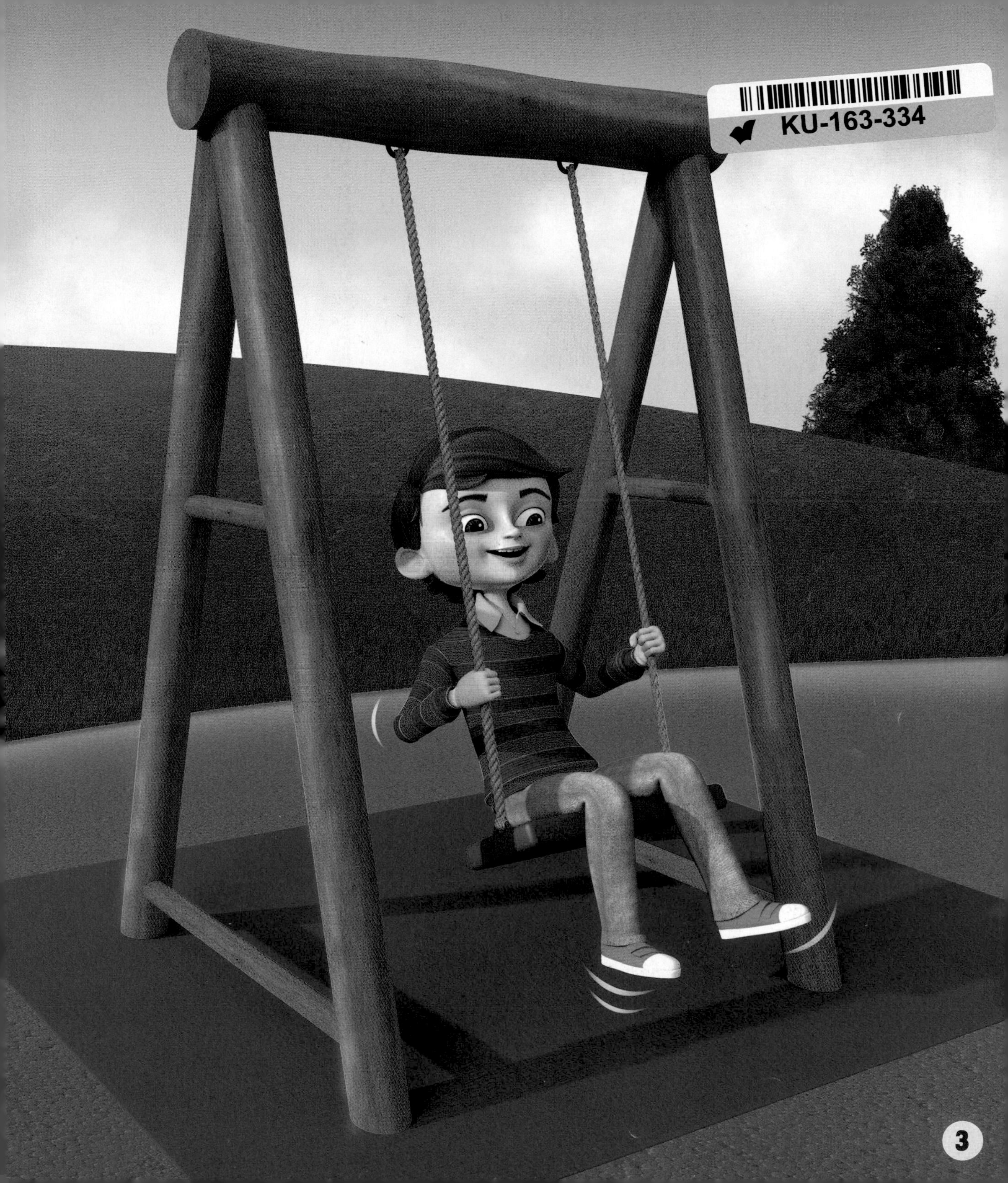

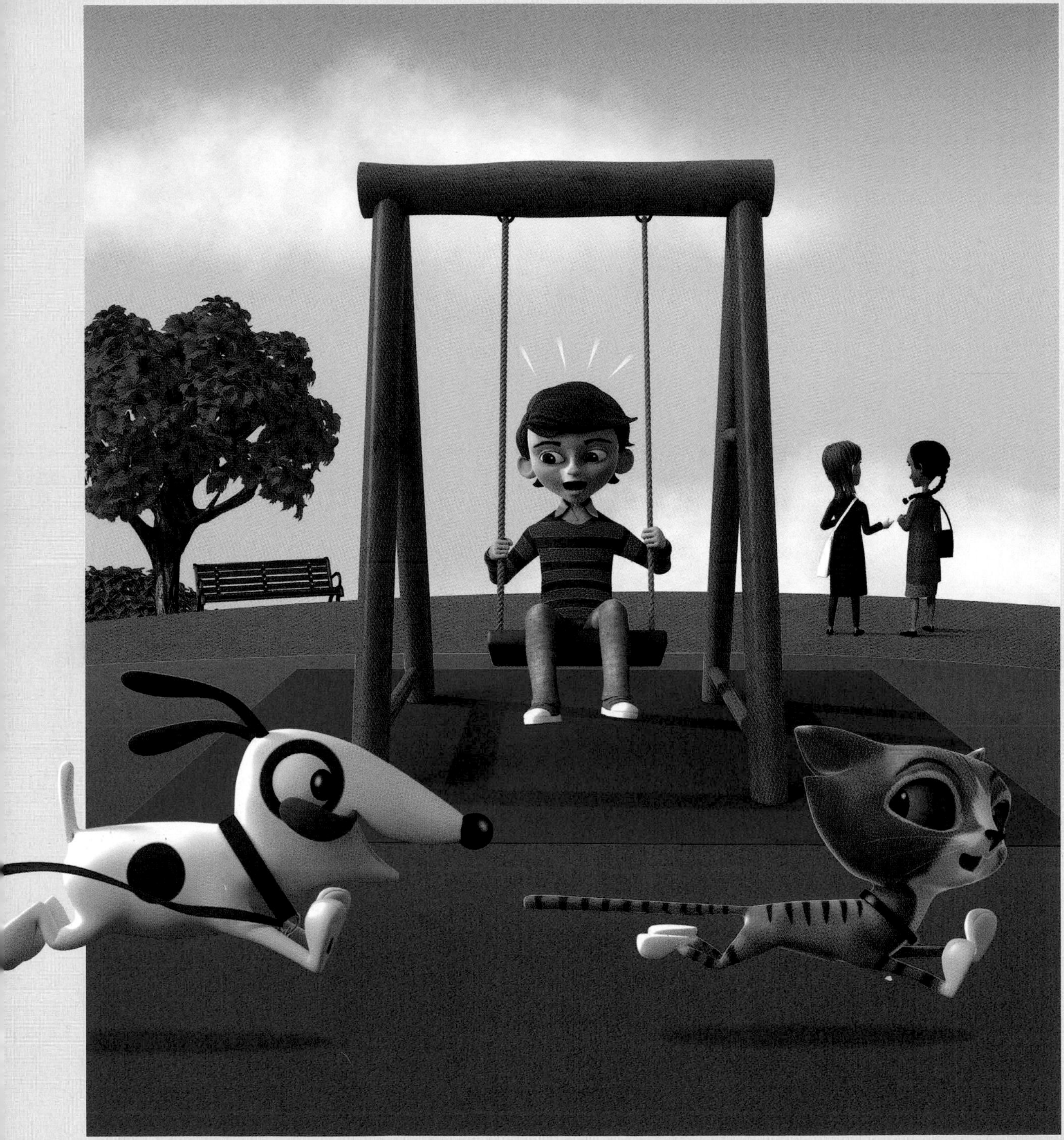

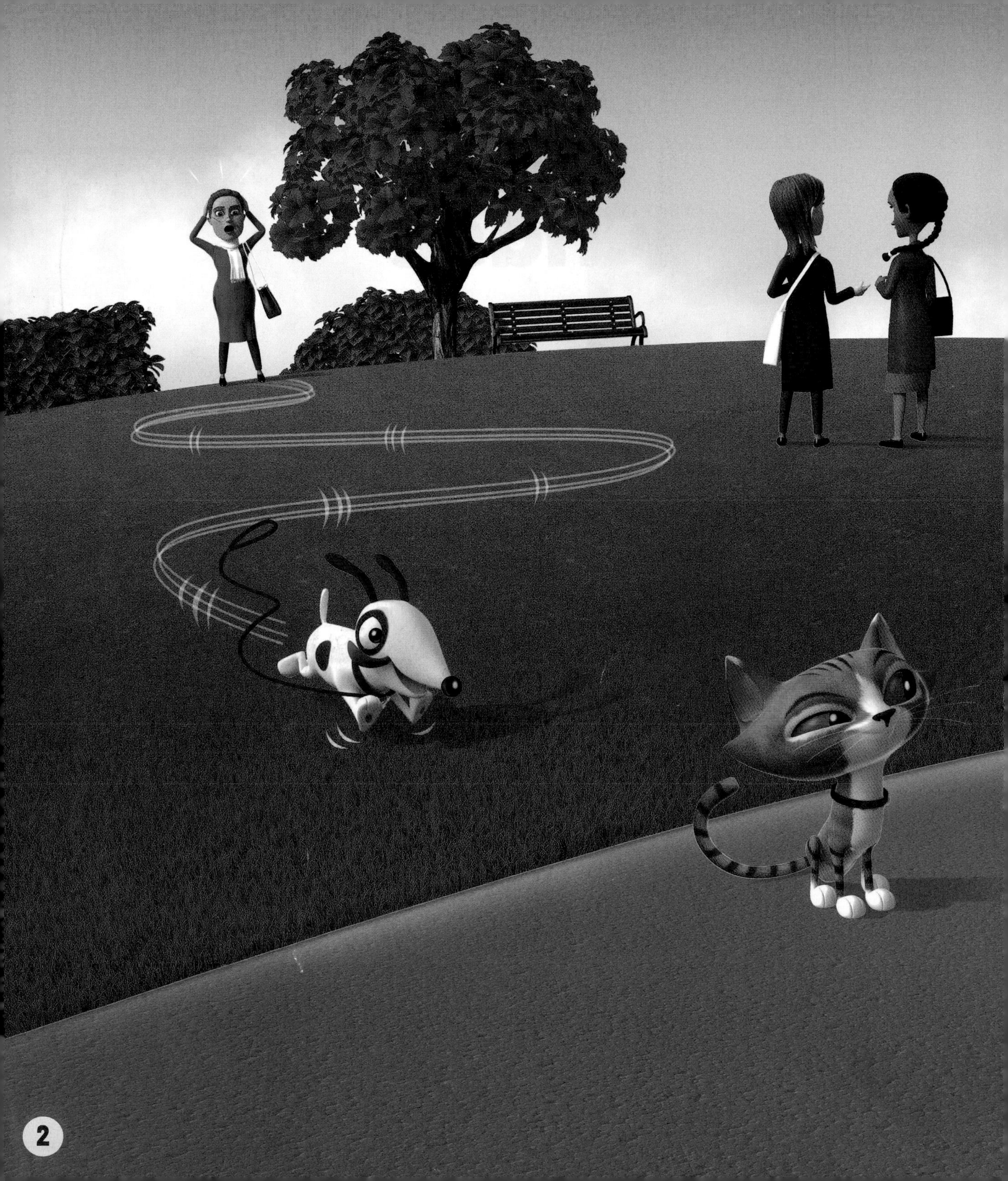

Cat
Cl

by
Illustrat

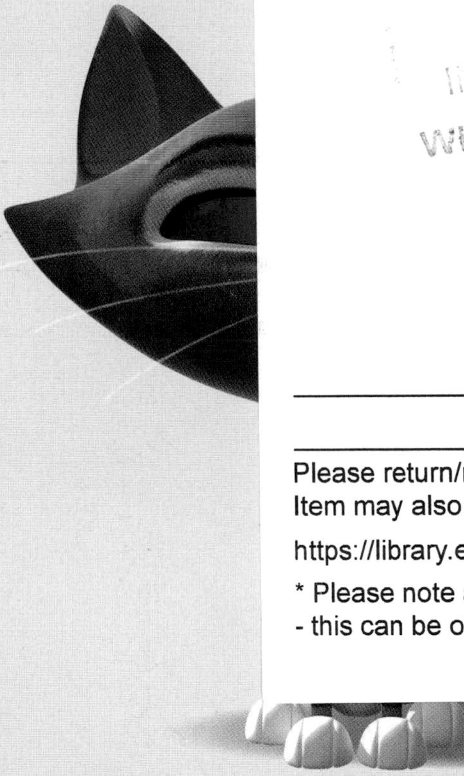

OXFORD
UNIVERSITY PRESS

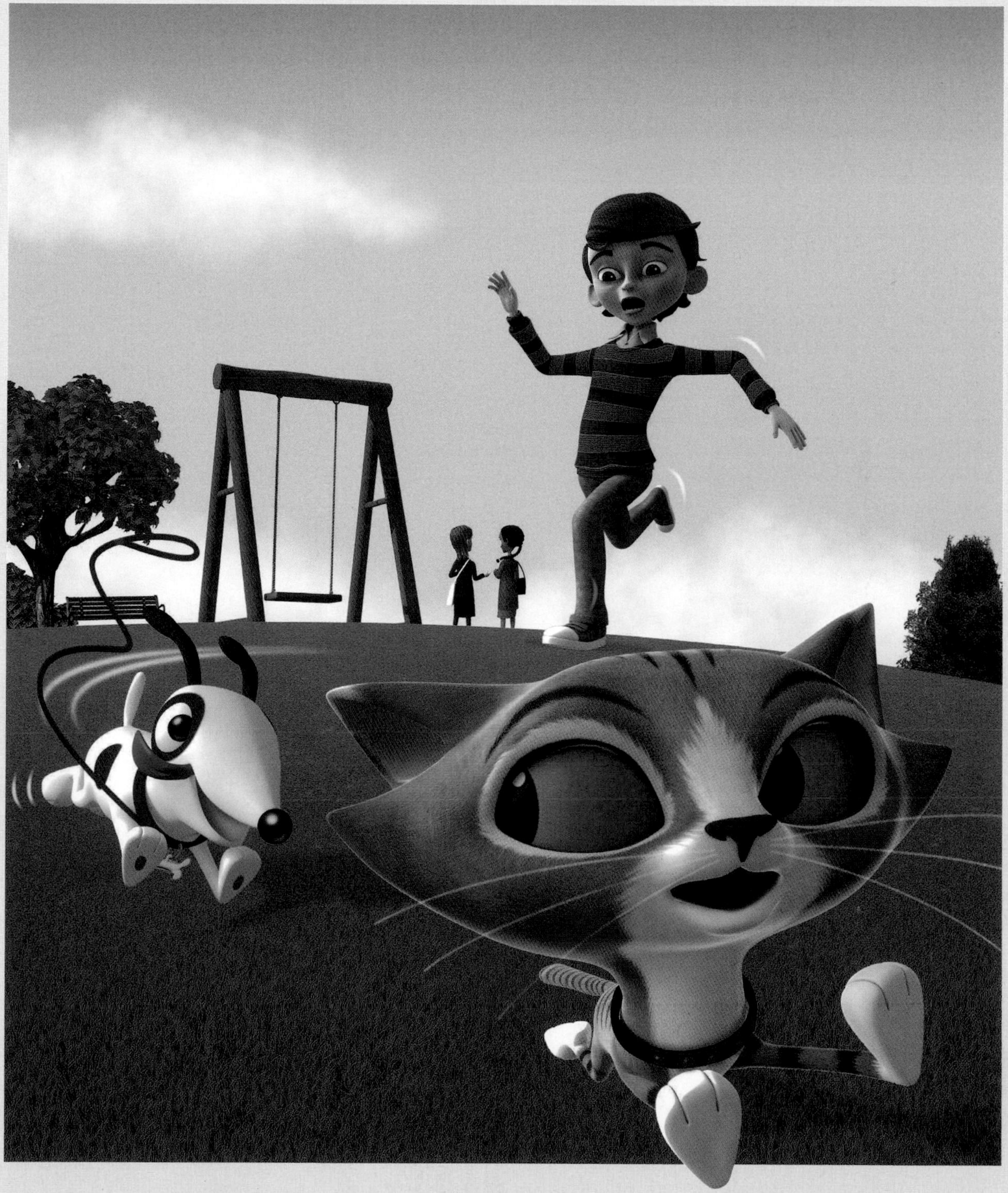

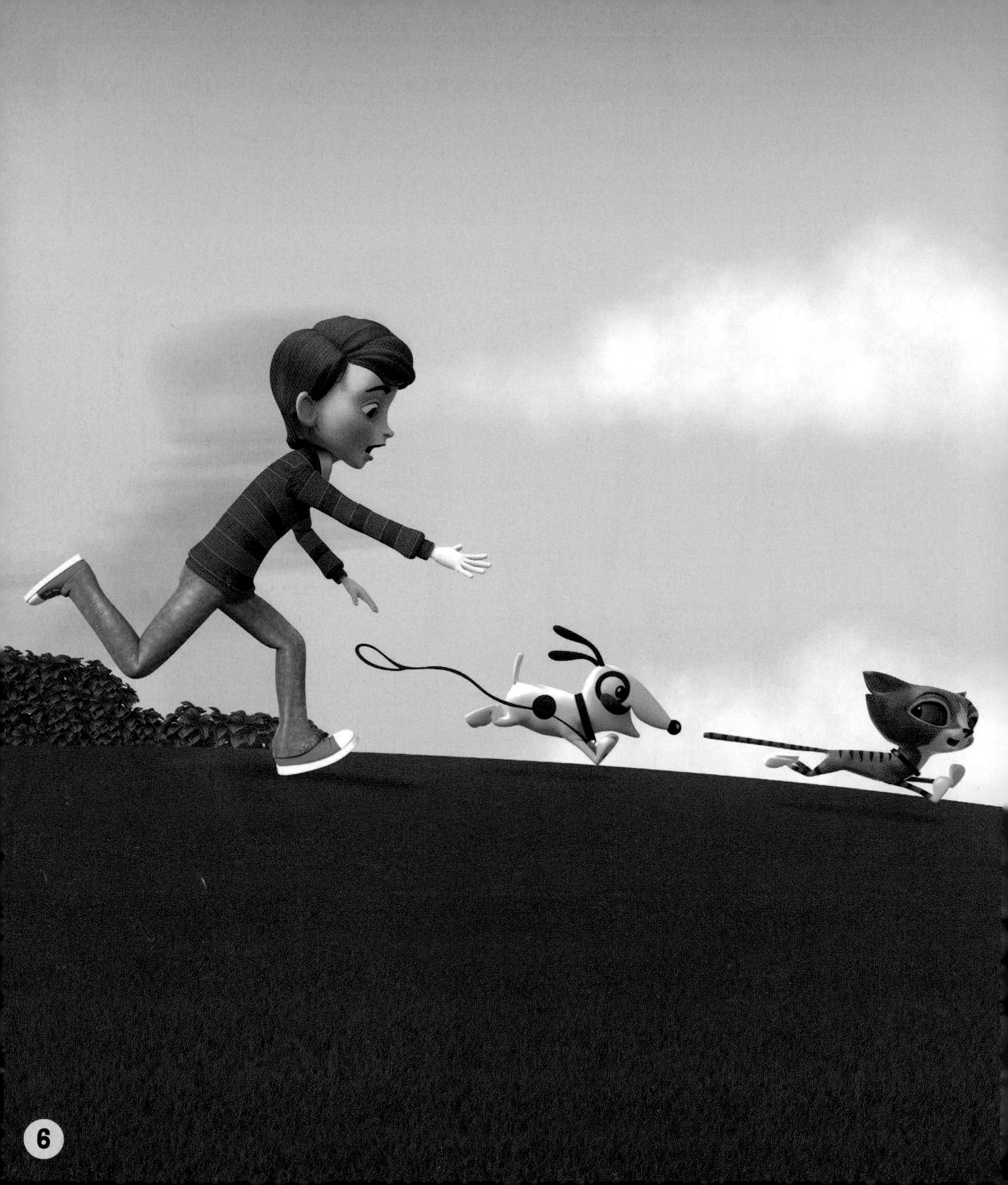

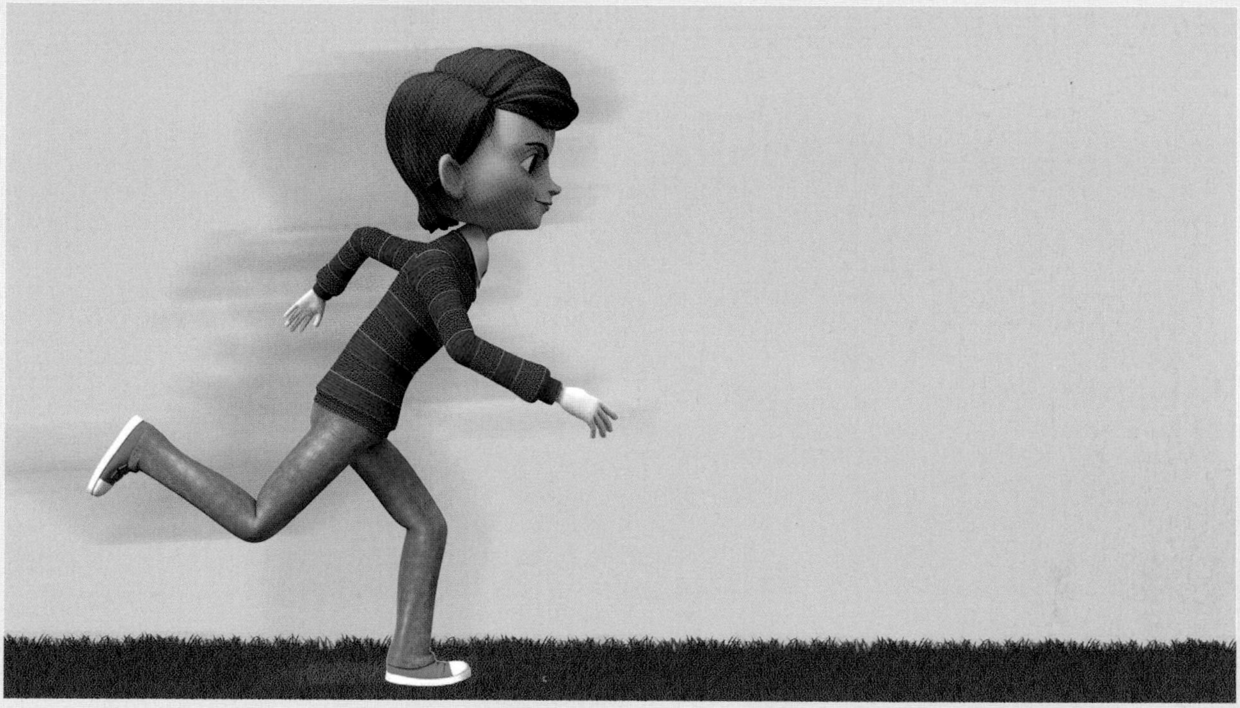

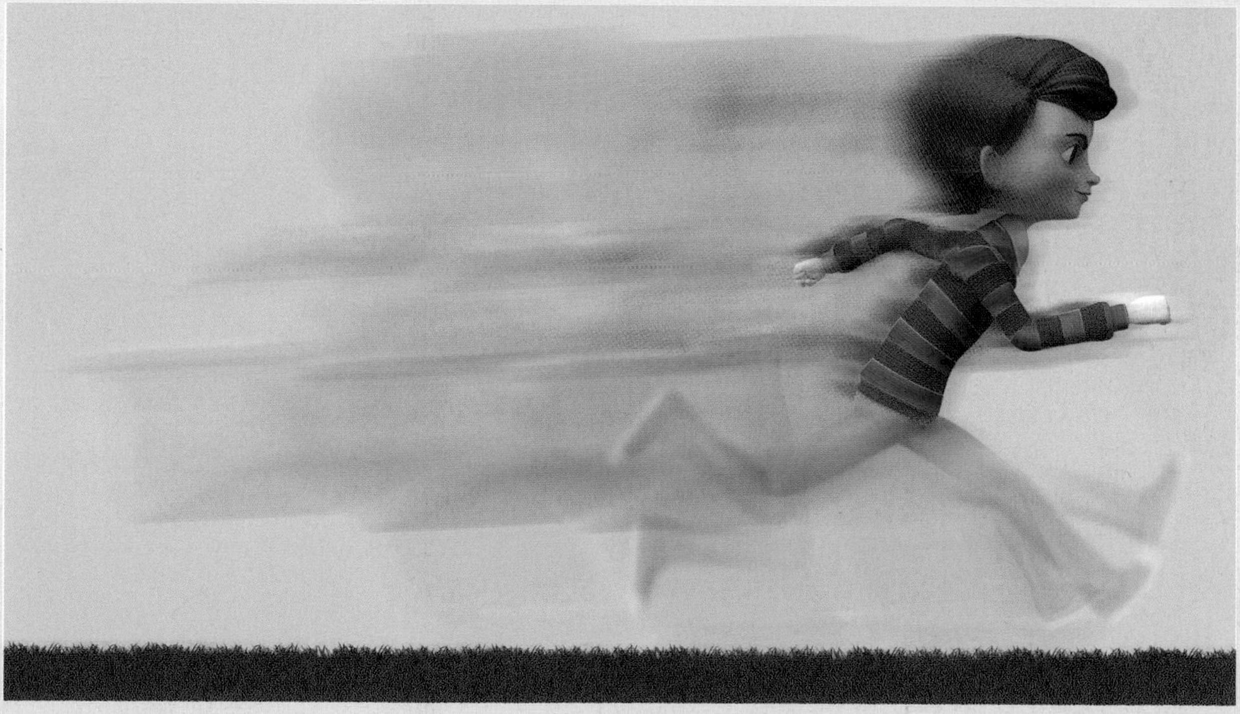

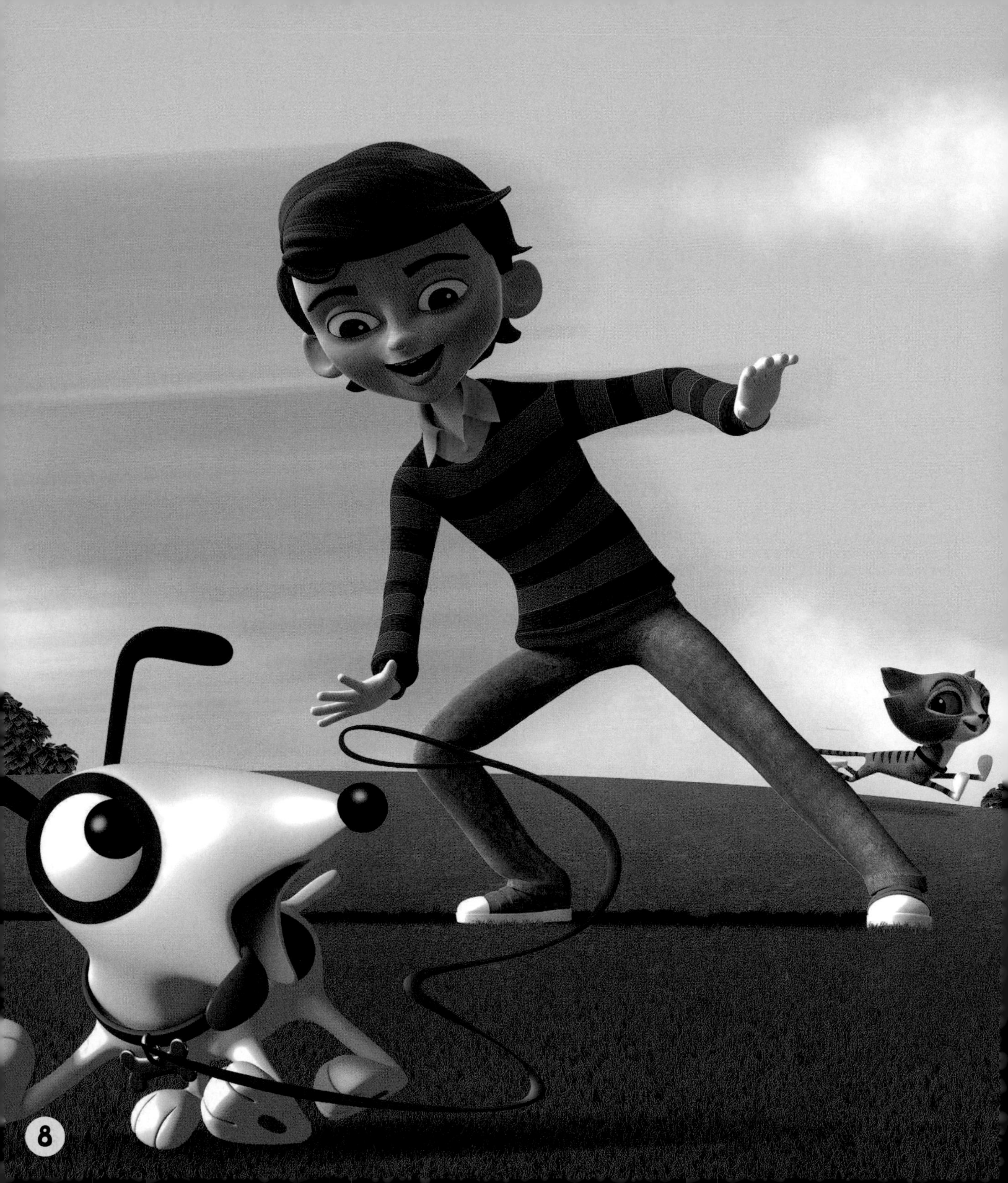

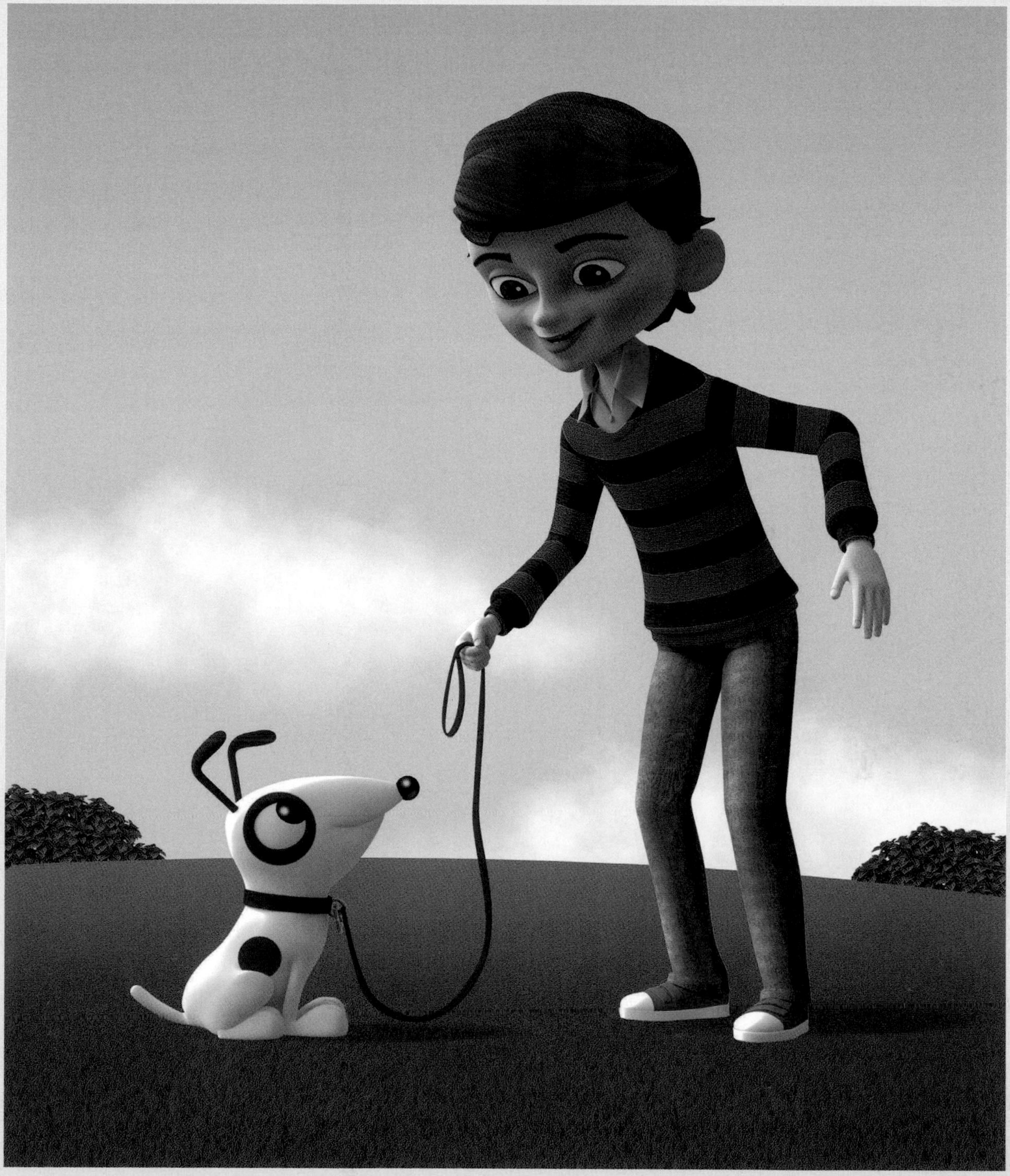

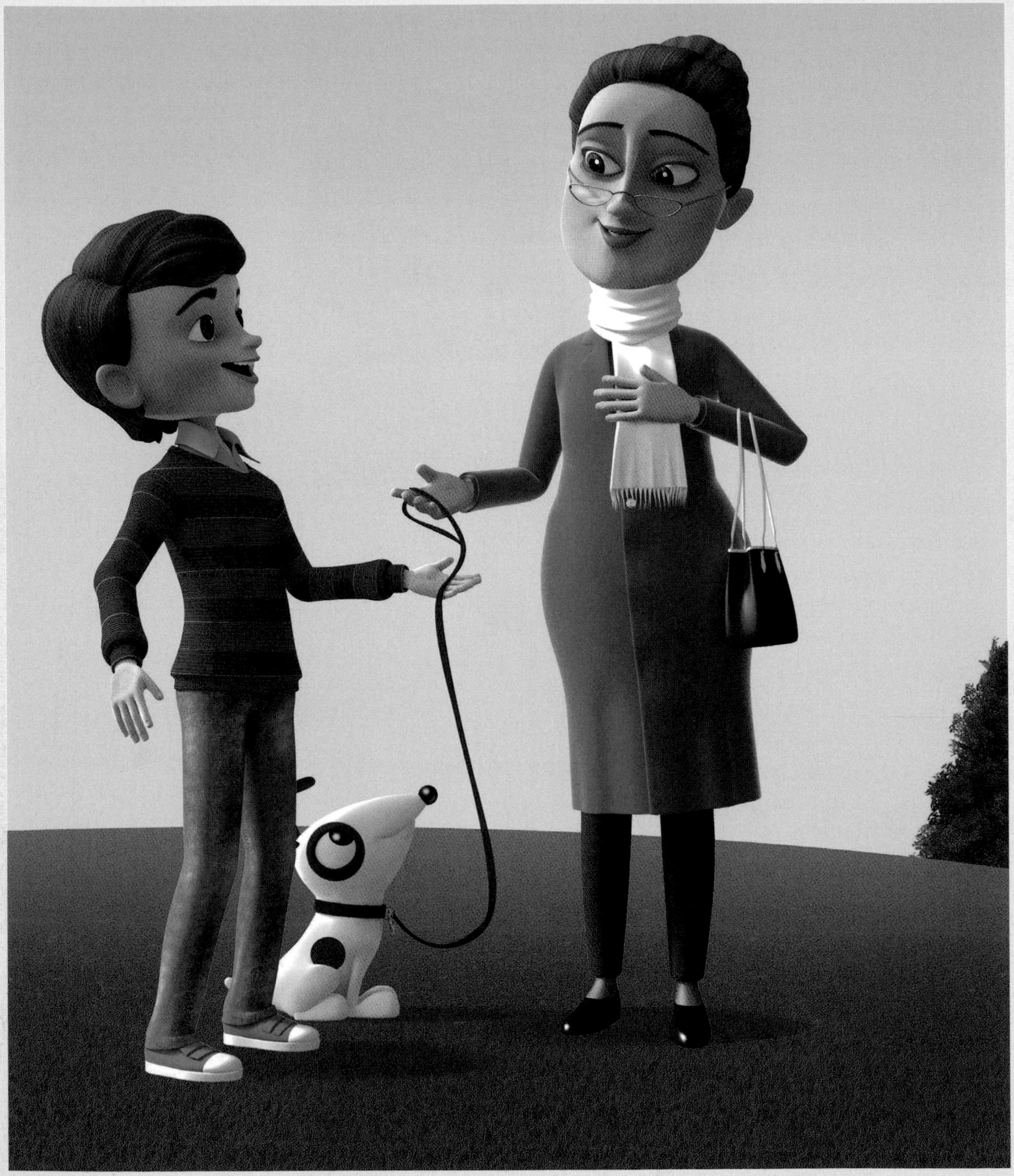

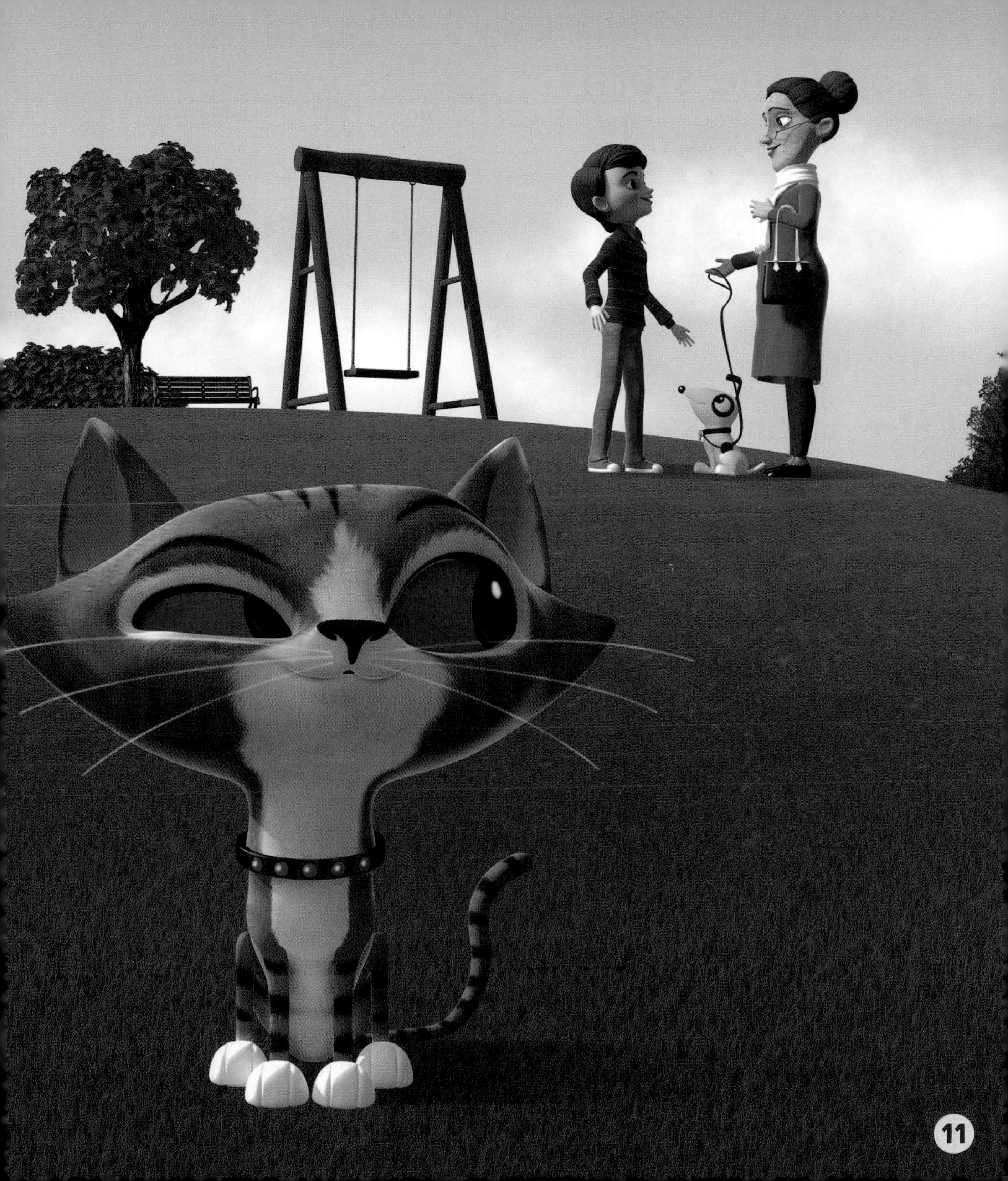

Retell the story ...

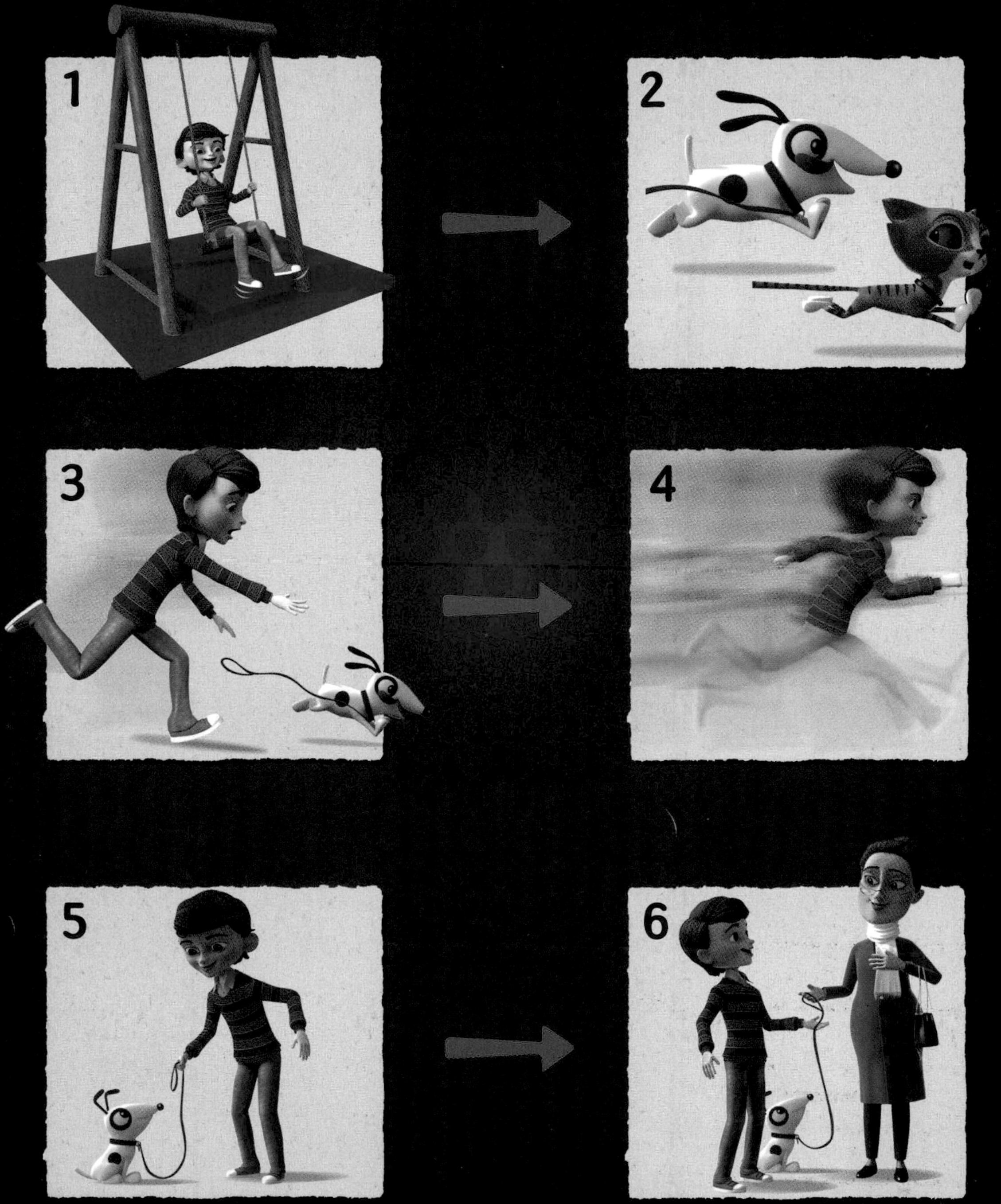